THE HIDDEN PATH TO ETHICAL SUSTAINABILITY

CRAFTING A GREENER TOMORROW

DR. MINAKSHI BANSAL

Contents

Contents

Prayer

"Om Bhadram Karnebhih Shrinuyama Devah
Bhadram Pashyemakshabhiryajatrah
Sthirairangais Tushtuvamsastanubhih
Vyashema Devahitam Yadayuh
Svasti Na Indro Vriddhashravah
Svasti Nah Pusha Vishwavedah
Svasti Nastarkshyo Arishtanemih
Svasti No Brihaspatir Dadhatu
Om Shantih Shantih Shantih"

This mantra is a prayer for universal well-being, invoking the blessings of various deities for protection, health, and happiness. It emphasizes the importance of experiencing the auspicious through all senses and living a life aligned with divine purpose. The repetition of "Shantih" at the end signifies a deep desire for peace in the individual, the environment, and the universe at large. This mantra is often recited as a prayer for peace, prosperity, and the physical and spiritual well-being of all beings.

ɮɮɮ

About The Author

Dr. Minakshi Bansal, born in the bustling metropolis of Delhi, India, has led a life steeped in artistry, scholarly pursuit, and an unwavering commitment to societal betterment. Following her marriage, she relocated to Ahmedabad, Gujarat, where she has since blossomed into a multifaceted beacon of inspiration for many. Dr. Minakshi is not only recognized as a gifted artist in the realm of Fine Arts but also as an esteemed author, a devoted social worker and a dedicated research scholar in Psychology. Her journey, marked by a profound dedication to elevating those around her, especially the downtrodden and underprivileged children of society, is a testament to her deep-seated belief in the transformative power of engagement and empathy.

From her earliest days, Minakshi was distinguished by an insatiable appetite for reading. Her literary universe was inhabited by characters and narratives that spanned ethical tales, motivational and inspirational stories, and the mythic parables imbued with life lessons. This voracious reading habit was not merely for personal edification but was driven by a desire to distill and disseminate the essence of these narratives to foster the development of students and peers alike. She was particularly captivated by the lives and teachings of historical figures and spiritual leaders such as Adi Shankaracharya, Swami Vivekananda, Dr. APJ Abdul Kalam, Mahamana Pandit Madan Mohan Malviya, Mahatma Gandhi, Sardar Vallabhai Patel, and Vinoba Bhave, among others. Their philosophies and life stories fueled her ambition to embody their ideals of resilience, selflessness, and relentless pursuit of knowledge.

Dr. Minakshi's academic and practical engagement with psychology has been equally noteworthy. As a research scholar, her focus has been on exploring the intricate tapestry of the human psyche, aiming to unlock the potential for psychological well-being and societal harmony. Her scholarly work is complemented by her active involvement in social work, where she employs her academic insights to make tangible differences in the lives of the underprivileged. Her endeavours in social work are characterized by an innovative approach that combines traditional wisdom with contemporary psychological practices to address the multifaceted challenges faced by these communities.

Her artistic talents, another facet of her diverse capabilities, are not merely a personal passion but also serve as a medium through which she communicates and connects with others. Her art, rich in symbolism and emotional depth, reflects her philosophical inquiries and social concerns, offering viewers a glimpse into the breadth of her intellect and the depth of her compassion.

In addition to her contributions to the arts and social sciences, Dr. Minakshi has embraced the healing arts of Pranic Healing, mastering the techniques developed by Master Choa Kok Sui. This practice, which focuses on the manipulation of Prana or life energy to heal the body and aura, has been both a personal journey of discovery and a means through which she extends her healing touch to others. Her proficiency in Pranic Healing is complemented by her advocacy and teaching of various forms of meditation aimed at rejuvenation, personal betterment, and the cultivation of harmony within individuals and communities alike.

Dr. Minakshi's life is a narrative of relentless pursuit, not just of personal achievement but of the upliftment and empowerment of society at large. Her diverse interests and talents—spanning the arts, literature, psychology, and the healing practices—converge on a singular path of service. She embodies the spirit of the luminaries who inspired her, channelling their legacy through her actions and teachings. Through her books, art, and social initiatives, she continues to inspire a new generation to embark on their own journeys of self-discovery, resilience, and altruism.

Her commitment to social betterment, particularly her focus on uplifting underprivileged children, reflects a deep understanding of the transformative potential of education and personal development. By integrating her knowledge of psychology, her artistic sensibilities, and her healing practices, Dr. Bansal has developed a holistic approach to social work that addresses both the immediate needs and the long-term well-being of the communities she serves.

As an author, Dr. Minakshi's writings offer a blend of inspirational insights, practical wisdom, and reflective contemplations drawn from her extensive reading and life experiences. Her books serve as a guide for those seeking to navigate the complexities of life with grace, resilience, and purpose. Through her narratives, she extends an invitation to her readers to explore the depths of their own potential and to contribute meaningfully to the collective well-being of society.

In Dr. Minakshi Bansal, we find a remarkable synthesis of the artist, the scholar, the healer, and the social activist. Her life's work stands as a beacon of hope and a source of inspiration for individuals seeking to make a difference in the world. Her story is a compelling reminder of the power of individual action, rooted in compassion and driven by a profound commitment to the betterment of humanity. Dr. Minakshi's legacy is not just in the tangible outcomes of her efforts but in the enduring spirit of inquiry, empathy, and service that she embodies.

❦❦❦

Preface

In crafting a greener tomorrow, the journey we embark on is neither straightforward nor simple. It requires a deep rethinking of how we interact with our world—a profound shift from exploitation to cooperation, from short-term gains to long-term well-being. This book is born out of the belief that sustainability must be woven into the very fabric of our existence, and that the ethical considerations of our environmental impact are as crucial as the physical ones.

As we stand at a critical juncture in our planetary history, faced with daunting challenges of climate change, resource depletion, and widespread ecological degradation, the imperative to act is urgent. However, action without ethical grounding is like a ship sailing without a compass. It is with this perspective that I delve into the concept of ethical sustainability, exploring its nuances and its vital importance in our efforts to secure a viable future for ourselves and subsequent generations.

The principles of ethical sustainability are not merely academic; they are actionable mandates that can and should inform every aspect of our daily lives and societal structures. From the way we grow our food and generate our power to how we design our cities and run our economies, there is an undeniable need to infuse sustainability with a strong ethical framework. This book aims to illuminate the often hidden paths that individuals, communities, and nations can take to achieve this integration.

The chapters within this book explore various dimensions of ethical sustainability, each addressing specific elements such as renewable energy, sustainable agriculture, water conservation, and waste management. These topics are familiar in the discourse on sustainability, yet this exploration goes a step further by intertwining ethical considerations directly into each discussion.

What does it mean to pursue renewable energy if the means of obtaining it impinge upon the rights and lands of indigenous populations? How can we claim to support sustainable agriculture if the workers on these farms are not ensured fair wages and safe working conditions? These are some of the critical questions this book addresses.

Moreover, the role of technology and innovation is discussed not just in terms of ecological benefits but also in the broader context of social and economic impacts. It is vital that our push for innovation is not at the expense of ethical considerations but rather is aligned with creating solutions that benefit all segments of society equitably. This includes ensuring that the fruits of innovation do not exacerbate existing inequalities but instead contribute to rectifying them.

This narrative also challenges the traditional corporate and governmental pathways that have often favored economic growth at a detrimental cost to the environment. It advocates for a new model of leadership and governance that prioritizes the long-term health of the planet over immediate financial gains. The discussions highlight the importance of global cooperation and partnerships, stressing that the environmental crises we face are bound by no borders and can be effectively addressed only through collective international efforts.

In addition, the book does not shy away from the cultural dimensions of sustainability. It delves into how our arts, media, and broader cultural expressions shape and are shaped by our environmental practices. It posits that cultural transformation is a cornerstone of sustainable change, capable of fostering a deeper, more personal connection to environmental ethics.

As the author, my goal is to inspire, educate, and mobilize readers towards embracing ethical sustainability. The task is indeed great, and the paths are complex, but the vision of a greener tomorrow is clear and attainable. Through this book, I invite you to reflect, question, and act on the principles discussed, integrating them into your personal lives and wider community interactions.

Ultimately, the future we craft—this greener, more ethical tomorrow—will be a testament to our collective resolve to respect and protect the planet that sustains us all. It is a future that we must approach with both determination and humility, aware of the challenges but inspired by the possibilities that ethical sustainability holds. Let this book serve as both a guide and an invitation to join in this crucial endeavor.

Dr. Minakshi Bansal
Social Activist
Ahmedabad, Gujarat, Bharat

PPP

ONE

THE FOUNDATION OF ETHICAL SUSTAINABILITY

The journey towards a sustainable future is rooted deeply in the principles of ethical sustainability, which emphasizes the interconnection between environmental stewardship, equitable resource distribution, and moral responsibility. Ethical sustainability goes beyond the simple notion of reducing environmental impacts; it involves a comprehensive approach to managing the Earth's resources in a manner that is fair, equitable, and mindful of future generations. This concept is built on the understanding that our actions today have far-reaching consequences on the planet and its inhabitants, prompting a need for a shift in how we perceive and interact with our environment.

Central to the idea of ethical sustainability is the principle of intergenerational equity, which argues that we have a moral obligation to preserve the environment in a state that will allow future generations to enjoy the same natural resources and beauty that we do today. This principle challenges the current exploitation-based model of economic growth, which often leads to resource depletion, environmental degradation, and increased inequality. By adopting a sustainability framework that respects and integrates ethical considerations, we can create a balanced approach that promotes environmental health, social equity, and economic viability.

Another cornerstone of ethical sustainability is the concept of ecological integrity. This concept stresses the importance of maintaining the diverse systems and processes of the natural world. Healthy ecosystems are vital for the survival of all species, including humans, as they provide essential services such as clean air and water, pollination of plants, and regulation of the climate. To uphold ecological integrity, it is crucial to adopt practices that protect these systems from harm and allow them to function naturally. This includes reducing pollution, conserving habitats, and restoring areas that have been damaged by human activity.

Transparency and accountability also play critical roles in the foundation of ethical sustainability. For sustainability efforts to be effective, they must be transparent and subject to scrutiny. This openness encourages public participation and ensures that decisions are made in the best interest of the community and the environment. Accountability mechanisms, such as environmental impact assessments and sustainability audits, help ensure that individuals, companies, and governments adhere to environmental laws and commitments. By fostering a culture of accountability, we can prevent environmental abuses and promote practices that contribute to a sustainable future.

Inclusion is also a fundamental aspect of ethical sustainability. This involves ensuring that all voices, particularly those of marginalized and indigenous communities, are heard in the planning and implementation of sustainability projects. These communities are often the most affected by environmental degradation and climate change, yet they typically have the least amount of power in decision-making processes. Inclusion not only leads to fairer outcomes but also enriches sustainability initiatives by incorporating diverse perspectives and knowledge, particularly traditional practices that have been sustainable over centuries.

By understanding and integrating these principles, we can lay a solid foundation for ethical sustainability. This foundation supports the development of policies, practices, and behaviors that not only protect the environment but also promote social justice and economic development. As we move forward, it is crucial that individuals, businesses, and governments consider the ethical implications of their actions and strive to make decisions that benefit both the planet and its people.

Transitioning to the subsequent elements of sustainability, the journey expands from foundational ethics to practical applications in various sectors, demonstrating the pervasive nature of sustainability in achieving a balanced and equitable future.

ppp

"True sustainability goes beyond reducing emissions; it integrates justice and ethics into the very fabric of our decision-making processes, ensuring a balanced approach to environmental stewardship."

ɒɒɒ

TWO
EVALUATING OUR ENVIRONMENTAL FOOTPRINT

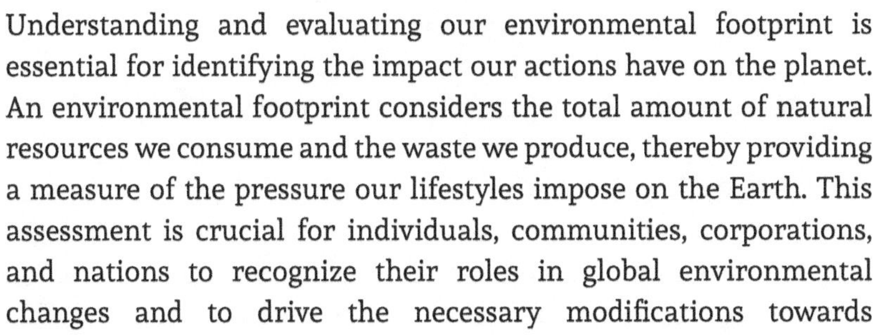

Understanding and evaluating our environmental footprint is essential for identifying the impact our actions have on the planet. An environmental footprint considers the total amount of natural resources we consume and the waste we produce, thereby providing a measure of the pressure our lifestyles impose on the Earth. This assessment is crucial for individuals, communities, corporations, and nations to recognize their roles in global environmental changes and to drive the necessary modifications towards sustainability.

The environmental footprint is typically divided into several categories, including carbon, water, and waste footprints, each highlighting different aspects of environmental impact. The carbon footprint measures the total greenhouse gas emissions caused directly and indirectly by an individual or group. This includes emissions from burning fossil fuels for electricity, heating, transportation, and the production of goods and services consumed. Reducing the carbon footprint is vital in combating climate change and involves transitioning to renewable energy sources, enhancing energy efficiency, and adopting cleaner transportation options.

The water footprint is another critical component, assessing the total volume of freshwater used to produce the goods and services consumed by an individual or community. It helps in understanding water use beyond direct consumption, incorporating the water used in the production process of various products, such as food and clothing. Addressing water footprint concerns involves implementing water-saving technologies, reducing water waste, and choosing products that require less water to produce.

The waste footprint examines the amount of waste generated, including solid and hazardous waste, and the effectiveness of waste management practices like recycling, composting, and landfill use. Minimizing the waste footprint requires a shift towards a circular economy, where products are designed to be reused, repaired, or recycled, thereby reducing the overall waste produced.

For businesses and governments, evaluating the environmental footprint can guide policy and decision-making. It can highlight areas where improvements are needed and help set specific, measurable targets for reducing resource use and emissions. This evaluation is often facilitated by tools such as Life Cycle Assessment (LCA), which examines the environmental impacts associated with all the stages of a product's life from cradle to grave.

At an individual level, understanding one's environmental footprint can lead to more conscious decision-making regarding daily habits, transportation choices, and consumption patterns. Simple actions like reducing meat consumption, choosing public transport, and avoiding single-use plastics can significantly reduce one's personal footprint.

However, the process of evaluating our environmental footprint also faces challenges, such as the availability and reliability of data, especially in less developed regions. Furthermore, there is often a lack of awareness or motivation among individuals and companies to change established behaviors and practices. Education and awareness campaigns are critical in overcoming these challenges, as they can increase understanding and encourage action towards reducing footprints.

Moreover, evaluating our environmental footprint must go beyond mere calculation to inspire real change. It requires integrating sustainability into the core values and operations of businesses and embedding environmental education into the curricula at all levels of schooling. Governments can support these efforts by creating incentives for sustainable practices and establishing strict regulations on waste management, resource use, and emissions.

As we delve deeper into the impacts of various industries and the effectiveness of different policies, the importance of a comprehensive evaluation of our environmental footprint becomes increasingly apparent. This evaluation not only highlights the current state but also charts a path forward, emphasizing the need for a collaborative approach to sustainability that includes stakeholders at all levels.

In moving towards more sustainable practices, the integration of footprint evaluation into regular operational, educational, and governmental frameworks continues to be a crucial step. This ongoing process is dynamic and requires continuous adaptation and commitment to achieve a sustainable balance between human activities and the planet's health.

$$\wp\wp\wp$$

"The future we strive for should not just be survivable, but equitable and vibrant; this is the promise of ethical sustainability, where every action is taken with consideration for its impact on both the planet and its people."

❧❧❧

THREE

RENEWABLE ENERGY: PATHWAYS TO A CLEANER FUTURE

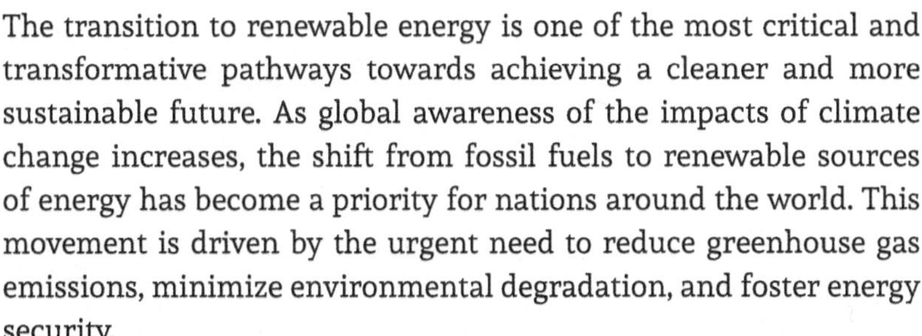

The transition to renewable energy is one of the most critical and transformative pathways towards achieving a cleaner and more sustainable future. As global awareness of the impacts of climate change increases, the shift from fossil fuels to renewable sources of energy has become a priority for nations around the world. This movement is driven by the urgent need to reduce greenhouse gas emissions, minimize environmental degradation, and foster energy security.

Renewable energy encompasses a range of technologies that draw power from natural processes that are continuously replenished, such as sunlight, wind, water flow, and geothermal heat. The most widely used renewable energy sources include solar, wind, hydroelectric, and geothermal energy, each offering distinct advantages and challenges, but collectively contributing to a sustainable energy landscape.

Solar Energy is one of the fastest-growing renewable technologies. It harnesses sunlight using photovoltaic cells to produce electricity. Solar energy is versatile, scalable from small, rooftop installations to large, ground-mounted solar farms, and is increasingly cost-effective due to technological advancements and economies of scale. The primary challenge with solar energy is its intermittent nature, as it generates electricity only when the sun is shining. However, innovations in battery storage technology are improving the ability to store solar energy for use during cloudy periods and nighttime.

Wind Energy is another major pillar of renewable energy strategies. Wind turbines convert the kinetic energy of wind into mechanical power, which can then be converted into electricity. Wind farms can be located on land or offshore, where they typically experience more consistent and powerful winds. The challenges associated with wind energy include visual and noise concerns, as well as the impact on wildlife, such as birds and bats. Despite these issues, wind energy remains a crucial component of the renewable energy mix due to its low operating costs and significant potential for expansion.

Hydroelectric Power utilizes the energy of water flowing from higher to lower elevations to generate electricity. This technology is one of the oldest and most mature forms of renewable energy. While hydroelectric facilities can provide large amounts of electricity and quickly adjust output to match demand, they can also have significant environmental and social impacts, including habitat disruption, changes to water flows, and displacement of local communities. As a result, the focus has shifted towards smaller, run-of-the-river projects that generate electricity without creating large reservoirs.

Geothermal Energy taps into the Earth's internal heat to generate electricity and provide direct heating. This can be achieved by harnessing natural geothermal hot springs or by drilling deep into the earth to access heat resources. Geothermal is highly reliable and can provide continuous, base-load power, unlike the more variable solar and wind resources. The main limitations of geothermal energy are its geographic dependency and the high initial costs associated with exploration and drilling.

The integration of these renewable technologies into the energy grid requires significant infrastructure and regulatory adjustments. Modern electrical grids need to be adapted to accommodate the variable outputs of solar and wind energy and to ensure reliability and stability of the power supply. This includes investments in grid modernization, such as smart grid technology, and improved forecasting methods for renewable production.

Governments play a crucial role in this transition by setting ambitious renewable energy targets, investing in research and development, and enacting policies that incentivize the adoption of renewables. Financial incentives, such as subsidies and tax credits, along with regulatory support, such as feed-in tariffs and renewable portfolio standards, are essential for accelerating the deployment of renewable technologies.

As the world increasingly moves towards renewable energy, the benefits extend beyond environmental impacts. Economically, the renewable sector represents a growing field that can create millions of jobs worldwide in manufacturing, installation, maintenance, and research and development. Socially, renewables contribute to energy security, reduce energy poverty, and can offer more decentralized and community-controlled forms of energy.

The transition to renewable energy is not merely a technical shift but represents a fundamental change in how societies produce and consume energy. As we continue to advance along this path, the role of citizens, businesses, and governments will be pivotal in shaping a sustainable future where energy production complements rather than compromises the health of the planet. The ongoing developments in renewable energy technologies and their integration into the daily lives of individuals around the world highlight the dynamic nature of this sector and underscore the potential for profound positive impacts on global sustainability efforts.

ႦႦႦ

"In the quest for a greener tomorrow, technology and innovation stand as beacons of hope, but must be guided by the moral compass of ethical sustainability to truly benefit humanity."

ᗺᗺᗺ

FOUR

SUSTAINABLE AGRICULTURE: FEEDING THE WORLD RESPONSIBLY

Sustainable agriculture is an evolving approach aimed at producing food in a way that maintains the health of ecosystems and supports the communities that depend on them. It represents a shift from the intensive, industrial methods that have dominated farming for decades, which often exacerbate environmental problems such as soil degradation, water scarcity, loss of biodiversity, and pollution. As the global population continues to grow, finding ways to feed the world without compromising the planet's health is more crucial than ever.

The core of sustainable agriculture lies in its capacity to integrate three main goals: environmental health, economic profitability, and social and economic equity. A variety of practices are employed to achieve these goals, including crop rotation, permaculture, agroforestry, integrated pest management, and the creation of genetically diverse agricultural systems. Each of these practices not only helps reduce the impact on the environment but also can improve food production and farmers' livelihoods.

Crop Rotation is a traditional farming practice that involves growing different types of crops in the same area across a sequence of growing seasons. It helps in maintaining soil health, reducing soil erosion, and preventing the build-up of pests and diseases that often occurs when one species is continuously cultivated. This practice can also improve soil fertility by planting legumes that fix nitrogen in the soil, which benefits subsequent plantings.

Permaculture is a design system for creating sustainable human environments. It is rooted in the observation of natural ecosystems and uses these as models for designing agricultural systems. Permaculture encompasses not just agriculture but also water management, energy conservation, and building design. Its principles are based on care for the earth, care for people, and fair share. By mimicking the no-waste, closed-loop systems seen in nature, permaculture aims at creating sustainable and self-sufficient agricultural practices.

Agroforestry combines agriculture and forestry technologies to create more diverse, productive, profitable, healthy, and sustainable land-use systems. Trees and shrubs are integrated with crops and livestock to create a symbiotic ecosystem. This method can help control temperature, reduce wind speeds, and increase biodiversity, which is beneficial for both crops and wildlife. Agroforestry not only conserves and protects natural resources but also provides diversified income through the harvesting of fruits, nuts, and timber.

Integrated Pest Management (IPM) is an approach to managing pests that combines biological, cultural, physical, and chemical tools in a way that minimizes economic, health, and environmental risks. IPM emphasizes the growth of a healthy crop with the least possible disruption to agro-ecosystems and encourages natural pest control mechanisms.

Diversifying agricultural systems is also a key element of sustainable agriculture. This involves cultivating a variety of crop species and strains within a given area, which helps to reduce crop failure and pest outbreaks while increasing local biodiversity. Such diversity also contributes to the nutritional diversity of the diet and provides a range of products that can be sold by farmers, reducing economic risk.

Implementing sustainable agriculture practices requires careful planning and commitment. It often involves changing existing farming methods, which can be challenging. However, the long-term benefits include increased farm productivity, reduced costs and dependency on chemical inputs, improved soil health, and greater resilience to environmental stressors.

Education and training for farmers are crucial for successful implementation. Farmers need to be well-informed about the benefits of sustainable practices and trained in new techniques. Moreover, government policies and incentives that support sustainable practices, such as subsidies for organic farming, can encourage more farmers to transition to sustainable methods.

Market support is also essential, as consumers increasingly seek out sustainably produced food. By creating and expanding markets for these products, the economic benefits of sustainable agriculture become more apparent to farmers.

As the global community looks towards solutions for sustainable development, agriculture continues to play a critical role. Not only is it a source of food and economic value, but it is also a potential means of mitigating climate change, conserving resources, and improving public health. By focusing on sustainable practices, we can support the health of our planet and ensure food security for future generations. The path forward involves collaboration among farmers, businesses, policymakers, researchers, and consumers all working towards a more sustainable agricultural future.

ᐅᐅᐅ

"Every drop of water saved, every kilowatt of renewable energy harnessed, and every policy enacted with equity in mind, moves us closer to a sustainable world that honors and protects all life."

ppp

FIVE

WATER WISDOM: CONSERVING OUR MOST PRECIOUS RESOURCE

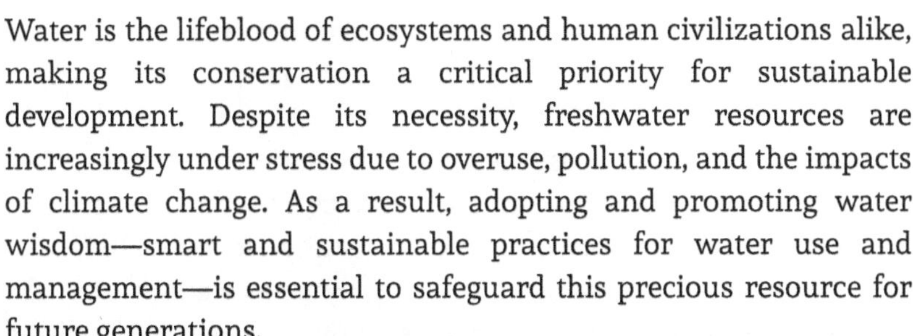

Water is the lifeblood of ecosystems and human civilizations alike, making its conservation a critical priority for sustainable development. Despite its necessity, freshwater resources are increasingly under stress due to overuse, pollution, and the impacts of climate change. As a result, adopting and promoting water wisdom—smart and sustainable practices for water use and management—is essential to safeguard this precious resource for future generations.

The conservation of water involves a variety of strategies and technologies aimed at reducing consumption, protecting water quality, and ensuring sustainable use. These strategies must be implemented at multiple levels, including individual, community, industrial, and governmental, to be effective. Each approach to water conservation helps mitigate the effects of water scarcity, supporting both human needs and environmental health.

Efficient Water Use starts with reducing wastage in domestic, agricultural, and industrial settings. In homes, water-saving fixtures such as low-flow toilets and showerheads, along with appliances like energy-efficient dishwashers and washing machines, can significantly reduce water usage. Communities can contribute by fixing leaks in public water systems, which can lose a substantial amount of water. Education and awareness campaigns are crucial in promoting these practices by making individuals aware of the importance of water conservation and the practical steps they can take.

Agricultural Water Management is vital as agriculture consumes more freshwater than any other source and wastes much of it through inefficiencies. Techniques such as drip irrigation and sprinkler systems target water directly to the roots of plants, minimizing evaporation and runoff. These systems can be automated to adjust for weather conditions and soil moisture levels, further enhancing water use efficiency. Additionally, the practice of capturing and storing rainwater for agricultural use can alleviate the pressure on freshwater sources.

Industrial Water Use also requires innovation and regulation. Industries can improve water efficiency by recycling used water for cooling processes or other non-consumptive uses. Advanced technologies, such as ultrafiltration systems, allow for the treatment and reuse of wastewater within industrial facilities, significantly reducing the demand for fresh water. Governments can facilitate these improvements through regulations and incentives that promote water stewardship in the industrial sector.

Protecting Water Quality is another fundamental aspect of water wisdom. Contamination of water bodies from agricultural runoff, industrial discharges, and urban waste poses severe risks to both human health and aquatic ecosystems. Strategies to protect water quality include stricter enforcement of pollution controls, investing in better sewage treatment facilities, and promoting practices that reduce chemical runoff into rivers and lakes. Buffer strips of vegetation along waterways can significantly reduce the amount of pollutants reaching a water body.

Sustainable Water Policies are necessary to address the complexities of water management in a changing climate. These policies should aim to balance water usage between different sectors and maintain the ecological health of water systems. This requires integrated water resources management (IWRM) approaches that consider the entire water cycle and involve all stakeholders in decision-making processes. Effective water governance is crucial for developing and enforcing policies that ensure equitable and sustainable water distribution.

Community-Based Water Management involves local populations in the planning and management of water resources. This participatory approach ensures that the solutions are culturally appropriate and technically feasible, leading to better sustainability outcomes. Communities that understand and have a stake in their water management are more likely to conserve and protect water resources diligently.

Technological Innovations in water conservation continue to emerge, offering new solutions to old problems. Smart water meters and sensors can provide real-time data on water use, detecting leaks and inefficiencies quickly. New water purification technologies, such as reverse osmosis and nanofiltration, can turn previously unusable water sources into potable water. The use of artificial intelligence and machine learning in predicting water usage patterns and optimizing water distribution systems also represents a significant advancement in water management.

As we face the challenges of limited freshwater resources, the wisdom of conservation becomes more apparent. It is not only about reducing water use but also about rethinking how we value and manage water. Promoting water wisdom is essential in all sectors of society, from the individual consumer to global policymakers. By embracing these practices, we can ensure that our most precious resource is preserved and protected, sustaining life and prosperity for generations to come.

ɊɊɊ

"Sustainable cities are not just about greener buildings and smarter infrastructure, but about creating spaces that nurture community, culture, and connection."

ppp

SIX

Waste Not: Innovations in Recycling and Reuse

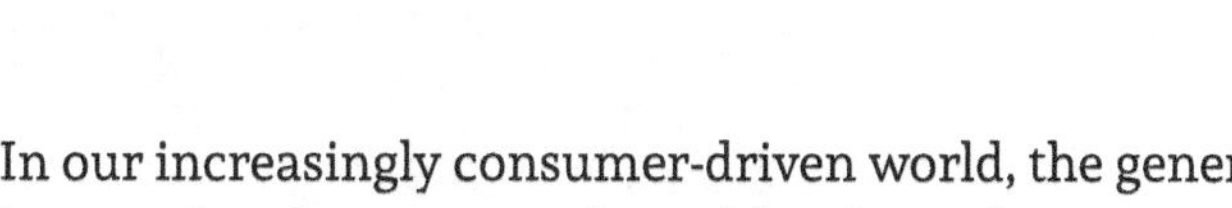

In our increasingly consumer-driven world, the generation of waste has escalated to unprecedented levels, with severe implications for the environment and public health. Addressing this challenge requires a shift towards more sustainable waste management practices, emphasizing innovations in recycling and reuse. These approaches not only help reduce the amount of waste sent to landfills but also conserve natural resources, reduce environmental pollution, and create economic opportunities.

Recycling: Closing the Loop on Waste

Recycling is a crucial component of waste reduction, transforming waste materials into new products to prevent the consumption of fresh raw materials. It involves several key processes: collecting and sorting waste, cleaning and processing it into raw materials, and manufacturing new products. Innovations in recycling technology have significantly improved the efficiency and effectiveness of these processes, allowing a broader range of materials to be recycled more thoroughly.

Advanced sorting technologies, such as single-stream recycling systems, enable consumers to place all recyclables into one bin. These materials are then separated using sophisticated machinery that can sort by material type, color, and even chemical composition. Optical sorting technology, for example, uses sensors to identify different types of materials based on how they reflect light, vastly improving the accuracy and speed of sorting recyclables from waste.

Enhanced Processing Techniques

Once collected and sorted, recyclable materials undergo processing to prepare them for manufacturing. Innovations in this area include new methods to clean and break down materials more efficiently. For instance, advanced mechanical recycling techniques have evolved to better process plastics, breaking them down into high-quality granules that can be used to produce new plastic products. These innovations help maintain the integrity and quality of recycled materials, making them more competitive with virgin materials.

Chemical recycling represents a significant advancement in dealing with hard-to-recycle plastics. Unlike traditional methods that melt plastic into a less pure form, chemical recycling breaks plastics down to their molecular level, allowing them to be remade into plastics of original quality. This process opens up recycling possibilities for more types of plastics, which were previously considered non-recyclable.

Promoting Reuse Over Disposal

While recycling is essential, reusing materials offers even greater environmental benefits by reducing the need to produce new products. Reuse initiatives have gained momentum through both grassroots movements and corporate strategies. Many communities host swap shops or repair cafes where individuals can bring items to be repaired or exchanged rather than thrown away. These initiatives help extend the life of products and reduce waste.

At the corporate level, many companies are shifting towards circular economy models, which emphasize keeping resources in use for as long as possible. For example, some companies have started offering products as a service, where consumers pay for the use of a product without owning it outright. This model encourages manufacturers to design for longevity, as the company retains ownership and responsibility for the product's maintenance and eventual recycling.

Zero-Waste Strategies

Zero-waste strategies aim to eliminate all discharges to land, water, or air that are a threat to planetary, human, animal, or plant health. In a zero-waste approach, waste materials are seen as potential resources that can be harnessed in closed-loop systems, similar to how natural ecosystems work. Many cities and businesses have adopted zero-waste goals, implementing comprehensive programs to reduce, reuse, and recycle materials.

Part of these zero-waste strategies involves developing new packaging solutions that reduce waste. Innovations include biodegradable packaging, refillable containers, and packaging-free stores where customers can bring their own containers. These efforts not only reduce the amount of packaging waste but also encourage consumers to think differently about waste and resource use.

Education and Participation

Education plays a pivotal role in successful recycling and reuse programs. Consumers need to be informed about what can be recycled or reused and how to properly sort and dispose of materials.

Many municipalities and organizations conduct educational campaigns to raise awareness and encourage participation in recycling programs.

Moreover, fostering a culture of sustainability within communities can lead to more effective and widespread adoption of waste reduction practices. Community involvement in designing and implementing waste management strategies ensures that these initiatives are well-supported and tailored to the specific needs and capabilities of the community.

As we face the dual challenges of resource depletion and environmental degradation, innovations in recycling and reuse are more crucial than ever.

By advancing these efforts, we can transform our waste into a resource that benefits the economy, society, and the environment, creating a more sustainable future for all.

ᗡᗡᗡ

"Art and culture weave the narrative of
sustainability into the fabric of society,
transforming abstract environmental issues into
personal and community-driven action."

❧❧❧

SEVEN
Green Building: Designing Sustainable Spaces

Green building is an approach to architecture and construction that seeks to minimize the environmental impact of buildings while enhancing the health and comfort of their occupants. This approach incorporates the design, construction, operation, and end-of-life recycling of buildings with the goal of creating structures that are environmentally responsible and resource-efficient throughout their life cycle.

Integrating Sustainable Design Principles

The foundation of green building is the integration of sustainable design principles from the earliest stages of the design process. This includes site selection, orientation, and the design of the building envelope itself. Sustainable design aims to optimize the use of natural resources and enhance the building's environmental performance. Architects and designers strive to minimize the disruption of the natural environment and incorporate elements that support the local ecology.

For instance, the orientation of a building is planned to maximize natural lighting and heating, thereby reducing the need for artificial light and energy for heating. The building envelope, which includes the walls, roof, and windows, is designed to maintain energy efficiency. Materials for these components are chosen based on their thermal performance, durability, and environmental impact, such as recycled content and sustainability certifications.

Energy Efficiency and Renewable Energy Sources

A critical aspect of green buildings is their energy efficiency. This is achieved through a combination of advanced design strategies, energy-efficient appliances and systems, and the use of renewable energy sources. Green buildings often incorporate high-efficiency windows and insulation in walls, roofs, and floors. Such features reduce the loss of heat during winter and keep the building cool during summer.

Renewable energy sources, such as solar panels or wind turbines, are frequently integrated into green buildings to reduce reliance on non-renewable energy sources. These installations help buildings generate their own clean energy and can significantly reduce greenhouse gas emissions associated with conventional energy use.

Water Conservation Practices

Water conservation is another pillar of green building. Sustainable buildings employ a variety of strategies to reduce water consumption and manage water more efficiently. These include low-flow fixtures, efficient wastewater management, and the use of non-potable water for toilet flushing and landscaping. Rainwater harvesting systems are also commonly used in green buildings to collect and store rainwater for on-site use, reducing the demand for municipal water supply and decreasing the building's overall water footprint.

Materials and Resources

The selection of materials is fundamental in the construction of green buildings. Sustainable building materials are those that are sourced and produced in an environmentally friendly manner. These materials often include recycled content, are recyclable at the end of their life, and emit low levels of volatile organic compounds (VOCs). Additionally, the use of locally sourced materials reduces the environmental impacts associated with transportation and supports the local economy.

Construction waste management is also a critical component of green building. By planning for material optimization and on-site management strategies, construction waste can be significantly reduced. Materials can be recycled and reused, and waste diversion from landfills becomes a feasible and encouraged practice.

Indoor Environmental Quality (IEQ)

Green buildings prioritize indoor environmental quality to enhance occupant comfort and health. This includes the use of materials that are non-toxic and emit low VOCs, ensuring that indoor air quality is protected. Adequate ventilation systems are essential to reduce pollutants and maintain fresh air in the building. Natural light is maximized, and lighting systems are designed to be energy-efficient while providing sufficient visibility.

Certification Systems

Several certification systems have been developed to standardize what constitutes a green building. These include LEED (Leadership in Energy and Environmental Design), BREEAM (Building Research Establishment Environmental Assessment Method), and others.

These systems provide frameworks for assessing the performance of buildings in various categories such as energy efficiency, water usage, materials selection, and indoor environmental quality. Certification not only helps building owners and operators to evaluate the performance of their buildings but also provides a recognized standard that can enhance the marketability of buildings.

Green building represents a comprehensive approach to designing and constructing buildings that contribute positively to their environment. By focusing on sustainable design principles, energy efficiency, water conservation, material selection, and indoor environmental quality, green buildings can lead the way towards more sustainable development. As the world continues to face environmental challenges, the importance of green building in mitigating the impacts of climate change and supporting sustainable growth becomes increasingly evident.

ppp

"Global partnerships for environmental justice are not merely cooperative efforts; they are a testament to our shared destiny on this planet and our collective responsibility to nurture it."

ϸϸϸ

EIGHT

ETHICAL CONSUMERISM: MAKING MINDFUL CHOICES

Ethical consumerism represents a shift towards more conscious decision-making in purchasing practices, with an emphasis on the impact of these choices on the environment, human rights, and social justice. This movement encourages individuals to think about the broader consequences of their buying habits—such as the sustainability of resources, the treatment of workers in the supply chain, and the ethical practices of companies. As consumers increasingly seek to align their purchasing decisions with their values, businesses and markets are adapting, creating a dynamic interplay between supply and demand that fosters more sustainable economic practices.

Understanding Ethical Consumerism

Ethical consumerism is rooted in the idea that consumers can influence market trends and corporate behaviors by choosing to buy products and services that are ethically produced. This can include products that are made using sustainable practices, support fair labor conditions, avoid animal testing, reduce environmental impact, or contribute to social causes. The movement is not just about avoiding products from companies that engage in harmful practices; it's also about supporting businesses that are taking steps to improve.

The impact of ethical consumerism can be profound. When consumers choose to spend their money on ethically produced goods, they signal to businesses that there is a market for these products. This can encourage companies to assess and modify their practices, adopt sustainable manufacturing methods, and improve labor conditions. Conversely, boycotting products from companies that maintain harmful practices can pressure them to change to retain their customer base.

Challenges of Ethical Consumerism

While the concept of ethical consumerism is appealing, it presents several challenges. One of the main difficulties is the availability and accessibility of ethical products. In many regions, these products are not readily available, or they are priced significantly higher than their conventional counterparts, which can be a barrier for average consumers. Moreover, the lack of transparency and the prevalence of greenwashing—where companies mislead consumers about the environmental or ethical credentials of their products—can make it difficult for consumers to make informed choices.

To combat these challenges, education and awareness are key. Consumers need reliable information about the products they buy and the companies they support. This can be facilitated through labeling initiatives such as fair trade or organic certifications, which provide consumers with verified information about the ethical attributes of products. Additionally, the development of mobile apps and online platforms that rate the ethical practices of companies can help consumers make informed decisions even while shopping.

The Role of Businesses in Ethical Consumerism

Businesses have a critical role to play in the promotion of ethical consumerism. By adopting more transparent business practices and striving for certifications that validate their ethical claims, companies can build trust with consumers. This not only helps to differentiate their products in a competitive market but also fosters a loyal customer base that values ethical practices.

Furthermore, businesses can engage in corporate social responsibility (CSR) initiatives that go beyond basic compliance with ethical standards. These initiatives can include investing in sustainable technologies, supporting community projects, or advocating for policies that promote environmental sustainability and human rights. By doing so, businesses not only contribute positively to society but also enhance their own reputational capital.

Impact on Global Supply Chains

Ethical consumerism has the potential to transform global supply chains. As demand for ethically produced goods increases, there is a growing pressure on suppliers and manufacturers around the world to adopt more sustainable and humane practices. This can lead to improvements in working conditions, better environmental management, and more equitable business practices throughout the supply chain.

Consumers' growing awareness and demand for transparency have led to an increase in supply chain audits, third-party certifications, and direct sourcing models, where businesses work closely with suppliers to ensure compliance with ethical standards. These changes not only benefit workers and communities involved in the supply chains but also contribute to the long-term sustainability of the businesses themselves.

Fostering a Culture of Ethical Consumerism

To foster a culture of ethical consumerism, it is essential to cultivate values of mindfulness, responsibility, and community engagement among consumers. Educational campaigns, community programs, and public discussions about the importance of ethical choices can help embed these values in everyday consumer behavior.

Moreover, collaborations between businesses, non-profits, and governments can amplify the impact of ethical consumerism. Such partnerships can help standardize ethical practices, develop more robust certification schemes, and create economic incentives for companies to adopt sustainable practices.

Ethical consumerism is about making mindful choices that reflect our values and the kind of world we want to live in. By choosing to buy ethically produced goods, consumers not only support sustainable business practices but also contribute to a larger movement towards social and environmental sustainability. As this movement grows, it has the potential to drive significant positive change, making ethical consumerism a powerful tool for achieving a more just and sustainable world.

ᐅᐅᐅ

"The strength of a community's commitment to sustainability can be seen in its smallest actions—the local markets, the neighborhood gardens, and the grassroots campaigns that forge lasting change."

❧❧❧

NINE

CORPORATE RESPONSIBILITY IN THE AGE OF CLIMATE CHANGE

As the impacts of climate change become increasingly evident across the globe, the role of corporations in addressing environmental challenges has never been more critical. Corporate responsibility in the age of climate change involves a transformative shift in how companies operate, integrating sustainability into their core business strategies and beyond mere compliance or public relations. This shift not only helps mitigate the effects of climate change but also positions companies as leaders in sustainable development, potentially leading to long-term economic benefits and improved stakeholder relations.

Understanding Corporate Responsibility

Corporate responsibility refers to the accountability that corporations have towards their stakeholders, including employees, customers, communities, and the environment. In the context of climate change, this means taking proactive steps to reduce carbon footprints, enhance energy efficiency, and support broader environmental initiatives. Companies are increasingly expected not only to minimize negative impacts but also to be part of the solution by innovating new technologies and practices that help combat climate change.

Strategic Sustainability

Strategic sustainability involves embedding environmental goals into the very fabric of company operations. This includes setting measurable and ambitious targets for reducing greenhouse gas emissions, transitioning to renewable energy sources, and minimizing waste. For many companies, this means rethinking supply chains, improving resource efficiency, and innovating product designs for better environmental performance.

The benefits of strategic sustainability extend beyond environmental impacts. Companies that adopt sustainable practices often experience reductions in costs, enhanced brand reputation, increased attractiveness to investors, and improved competitiveness in their industry. Moreover, sustainability initiatives can drive innovation by pushing companies to rethink how they create products and services.

Engagement and Transparency

Transparency is a key aspect of corporate responsibility, especially in how companies report their environmental impact. Stakeholders, including investors, customers, and regulatory bodies, are increasingly demanding greater disclosure on sustainability practices. Many companies now produce annual sustainability reports that detail their progress towards environmental objectives, carbon footprints, and other sustainability metrics.

Engagement involves not just reporting but actively participating in broader discussions about environmental sustainability. Companies can lead by example, setting industry standards and encouraging peers to follow suit. They can also engage with governments, non-profits, and community groups to support environmental legislation, fund sustainability projects, and educate the public about climate change.

Adaptation and Resilience

Adapting to climate change is another critical area of corporate responsibility. Companies must assess their vulnerabilities to climate-related risks, such as extreme weather events, rising sea levels, or changing regulatory landscapes. Building resilience into their operations can involve diversifying supply chains, investing in resilient infrastructure, or developing emergency preparedness plans.

For industries particularly vulnerable to climate impacts, such as agriculture, insurance, and real estate, adaptation strategies are not just optional; they are essential for survival. These strategies not only protect the company's assets but also secure jobs and support local economies that depend on corporate stability.

Innovative Solutions for Mitigation

Corporations have significant resources and capabilities to innovate solutions that mitigate climate change. This includes developing new technologies that reduce emissions, such as carbon capture and storage, or creating products that help customers reduce their environmental impact. For instance, the automotive industry is pivoting towards electric vehicles, which can significantly reduce transportation-related emissions.

Investment in research and development is crucial for these

innovations. By prioritizing sustainability in their innovation strategies, companies can not only help solve environmental challenges but also open up new markets and growth opportunities.

Collaborative Efforts

No single company can tackle climate change alone. Collaborative efforts are essential, involving partnerships between businesses, governments, NGOs, and academia. These collaborations can enhance the scalability of solutions, pool resources for greater impact, and align efforts across sectors and geographies.

Corporate responsibility in the age of climate change is a comprehensive approach that requires companies to integrate sustainability into their core operations, innovate new solutions, and collaborate with other stakeholders. The drive towards sustainability is reshaping corporate strategies worldwide, with companies recognizing that environmental responsibility is not only beneficial for the planet but also crucial for their own future success. As more corporations embrace this responsibility, their actions can contribute significantly to global efforts to mitigate and adapt to climate change, setting the stage for a more sustainable future for all.

 PPP

"Education for sustainability is about more than imparting knowledge; it's about inspiring a new generation to redefine what it means to live responsibly on this planet."

❧❧❧

TEN

COMMUNITY-LED CONSERVATION EFFORTS

Community-led conservation represents a powerful approach to environmental protection and sustainability. By placing the power of decision-making in the hands of local communities, this model leverages the intimate knowledge and vested interest of local populations in the preservation of their natural surroundings. These efforts are pivotal because they recognize the crucial role communities play in sustaining biodiversity and ensuring the health of ecosystems. By empowering local stakeholders, community-led conservation fosters a sense of ownership and responsibility that can lead to more sustainable and effective management of natural resources.

The Importance of Local Involvement

Local communities often have a deep-seated connection with their environment, developed through generations of interactions and dependence on natural resources. This connection provides them with unique insights into local ecosystems and the changes these systems undergo. Community-led conservation leverages this extensive local knowledge to design and implement conservation strategies that are well-suited to local conditions and cultural contexts. This local involvement is crucial for the long-term success of conservation initiatives, as it ensures that strategies are culturally appropriate, socially accepted, and therefore more likely to be maintained.

Building Capacity and Empowerment

Empowering communities starts with building capacity at the local level. This involves providing training, resources, and support to enhance the skills and knowledge of community members, enabling them to effectively manage conservation projects. Capacity building can include a range of activities, from educating community members on the importance of biodiversity to training them in the skills needed for sustainable natural resource management, such as wildlife monitoring, data collection, and enforcement of local conservation laws.

Supporting community-led conservation also means ensuring that communities have the legal and institutional frameworks needed to manage and protect their natural resources. This often requires changes in legislation or policy to recognize local management rights, provide communities with land tenure security, and enable them to benefit economically from conserving their environment.

Integrating Traditional Knowledge with Scientific Research

One of the strengths of community-led conservation is its ability to blend traditional ecological knowledge with modern scientific research. Many communities have a profound understanding of their local environment, gained through centuries of living in close proximity to nature. This knowledge includes insights into the behavior of local wildlife, seasonal cycles, and ecological indicators that might not be evident to outsiders.

Integrating this traditional knowledge with scientific conservation methods can enhance the effectiveness and relevance of conservation efforts. For instance, community observations can help identify critical habitats or changes in wildlife populations, which can then be verified through scientific studies. This integration not only enriches the data available for conservation efforts but also helps bridge the gap between modern science and indigenous practices, fostering mutual respect and collaboration.

Community-Based Resource Management

Community-based resource management (CBRM) is a practical application of community-led conservation. CBRM involves the management of natural resources by the people who live closest to them and are directly impacted by their conservation. This management approach can apply to a variety of resources, including forests, wildlife, water bodies, and fisheries.

CBRM schemes typically operate on principles of sustainable use and equitable distribution of resources. They aim to balance the ecological needs of the environment with the economic and social needs of the community. By involving community members in decision-making processes, CBRM helps ensure that conservation efforts do not just impose restrictions but also provide tangible benefits to local populations, such as improved livelihoods, which can decrease reliance on destructive practices like overfishing or illegal logging.

Success Stories and Scalability

There are numerous examples of successful community-led conservation projects around the world that have led to significant environmental improvements. For example, community-managed marine areas in the Pacific have successfully revived fish stocks by enforcing traditional fishing restrictions. In Africa, community wildlife conservancies have been instrumental in stabilizing populations of endangered species such as rhinos and elephants.

These successes demonstrate the potential for community-led conservation efforts to be scaled up and adapted to different contexts. However, scaling up requires careful consideration of the unique ecological, cultural, and socio-economic conditions of each new area. It also requires ongoing support from governments, NGOs, and other stakeholders to ensure that communities have the necessary resources and authority to manage their natural resources effectively.

Challenges and Future Directions

Despite their successes, community-led conservation efforts face challenges such as inadequate funding, political instability, and conflicts over resource use. Overcoming these challenges requires continued advocacy for community rights, increased investment in local conservation initiatives, and sustained efforts to integrate community-led conservation into broader environmental governance frameworks.

Community-led conservation is a vital strategy for preserving biodiversity and sustaining ecosystems. By empowering local communities to manage and protect their natural environments, these efforts harness local expertise and foster a deep-seated commitment to conservation that can lead to lasting environmental benefits. As the world grapples with escalating environmental challenges, community-led conservation offers a hopeful pathway towards more resilient and sustainable ecological management.

ᎮᎮᎮ

"As we innovate for the future, let us remember that technology serves us best when it serves our planet first, making sustainability not just an option but a guiding principle."

❧❧❧

ELEVEN

BIODIVERSITY AND ITS ROLE IN SUSTAINABILITY

Biodiversity, or biological diversity, refers to the variety of life on Earth—its species, habitats, and ecosystems, as well as the genetic diversity within species. This rich tapestry is not only a marvel of nature but also the foundation upon which human societies build their existence. Biodiversity plays a critical role in sustainability by maintaining ecosystem services that humans and all other life forms depend on. Understanding and preserving biodiversity is therefore central to sustaining our world's environmental health, economic prosperity, and social well-being.

The Ecological Importance of Biodiversity

Biodiversity supports complex ecosystems in which each organism, no matter how small, plays a specific role. These roles range from pollinating plants and cycling nutrients to providing food and regulating climate. The more biodiverse an ecosystem, the more robust it is against disruptions and the better it can maintain balance. For example, diverse plant species can support a wider array of animal species, thereby ensuring more stable food webs.

Ecosystem services, such as clean water, fertile soil, and a stable climate, are direct outcomes of these interactions within biodiverse systems. Forests, wetlands, and oceans, which are rich in biodiversity, are critical to carbon sequestration and storage, which mitigates climate change by absorbing carbon dioxide from the atmosphere. Similarly, diverse ecosystems help regulate water cycles and filter pollutants, ensuring clean and sustainable water sources.

Economic Benefits of Biodiversity

The economic implications of biodiversity are vast and often underappreciated. Many industries, such as agriculture, pharmaceuticals, and cosmetics, directly rely on a wide variety of biological resources. For instance, agriculture depends not only on crops and livestock but also on a variety of pollinators and soil organisms that enhance soil fertility and crop yields. Similarly, many pharmaceutical compounds are derived from the genetic material of wild species, with an estimated 50% of modern drugs developed from natural products.

Biodiversity also supports tourism and recreation industries, especially in areas where wildlife and pristine landscapes are major attractions. Eco-tourism and related recreational activities can generate significant economic benefits for local communities by creating jobs and supporting local businesses. Preserving biodiversity thus not only sustains these industries but also helps maintain the livelihoods of communities that depend on them.

Social and Cultural Dimensions of Biodiversity

Biodiversity is deeply intertwined with the cultural identity and well-being of many societies, particularly for indigenous and local communities who have developed sustainable ways of living that are closely aligned with the rhythms of their natural environments. Traditional knowledge systems, which have been honed over millennia, often include ways to use, manage, and conserve biodiversity effectively.

Cultural practices, rituals, and languages are often linked to particular species or landscapes. Loss of biodiversity can, therefore, lead to a loss of cultural heritage and identity. Furthermore, biodiversity in the form of diverse diets contributes to food security and nutritional health, which is crucial for overall social stability and well-being.

Threats to Biodiversity and Sustainability

Despite its importance, biodiversity is declining at an unprecedented rate due to human activities. Habitat destruction, pollution, climate change, overexploitation, and invasive species are among the primary threats to biodiversity. Each of these factors not only reduces biodiversity directly but also diminishes the ecosystem's ability to provide services that humans and other life forms rely on.

Addressing these threats requires concerted global, regional, and local efforts. Conservation strategies, such as protected areas and biodiversity corridors, are vital, but they must be complemented by sustainable management practices across all sectors of human activity. This includes adopting sustainable agricultural, forestry, and fishing practices that reduce impacts on biodiversity.

Future Directions for Biodiversity Conservation

Looking forward, the integration of biodiversity conservation into broader socio-economic planning and decision-making is essential. This involves recognizing the value of biodiversity in national and international economic accounting systems, integrating biodiversity considerations into trade regulations, and enhancing public awareness and education on biodiversity's importance.

Conservation efforts should also embrace innovative approaches such as biotechnology, which can help conserve genetic diversity, and ecological restoration, which aims to restore degraded ecosystems. Furthermore, enhancing the capacity of local communities to manage their natural resources through rights-based approaches can empower those who are most directly dependent on biodiversity for their survival and well-being.

Biodiversity is not merely an environmental issue but a comprehensive, multi-dimensional aspect of sustainability. Its conservation is crucial not only for the environment but also for economic stability and social justice. As the planet faces increasing environmental pressures, understanding and preserving biodiversity will be crucial to developing resilience against these changes and ensuring a sustainable future for all inhabitants of Earth.

ppp

"Ethical sustainability challenges us to rethink how
we value nature, urging us to see it not as a
resource to be exploited but as a partner in our
quest for a sustainable future."

ᐅᐅᐅ

TWELVE

THE IMPACT OF CLIMATE CHANGE ON MARGINALIZED COMMUNITIES

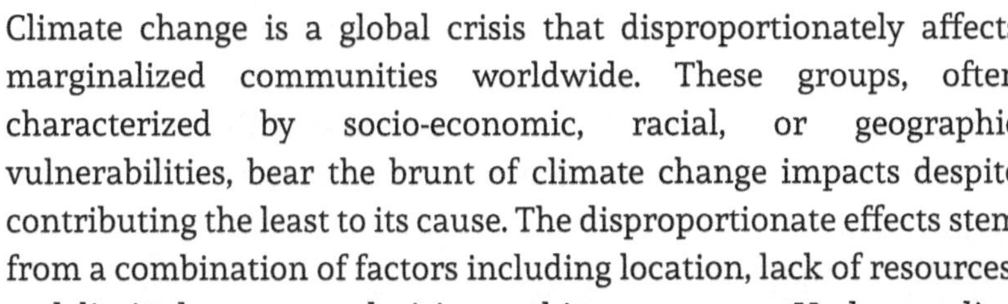

Climate change is a global crisis that disproportionately affects marginalized communities worldwide. These groups, often characterized by socio-economic, racial, or geographic vulnerabilities, bear the brunt of climate change impacts despite contributing the least to its cause. The disproportionate effects stem from a combination of factors including location, lack of resources, and limited access to decision-making processes. Understanding and addressing these impacts is critical to fostering resilience and ensuring equitable climate adaptation and mitigation strategies.

Vulnerability of Marginalized Communities

Marginalized communities are typically more vulnerable to the adverse effects of climate change due to several factors. Many such communities are located in areas highly susceptible to climate hazards, such as coastal regions prone to rising sea levels and storms, or arid areas susceptible to droughts. The infrastructure in these areas often lacks the resilience to withstand extreme weather events, leading to greater risk of disasters.

Economically, marginalized groups frequently have limited access to the resources necessary to adapt to climate change. This includes financial resources, land, water, and other critical assets. Socially and politically, these communities often have less influence over public policy and climate-related decision-making processes, resulting in a lack of adaptive public infrastructure and support systems that could mitigate climate risks.

Health Impacts

Climate change exacerbates health disparities among marginalized populations by increasing the prevalence of diseases, reducing access to clean water and food, and compromising healthcare infrastructure. For example, increased temperatures can lead to more frequent and intense heatwaves, which disproportionately affect those without adequate housing or cooling systems. Flooding and droughts compromise water quality and availability, leading to higher rates of waterborne diseases in communities

Economic Disparities

Climate-related events often cause significant economic disruptions, which can devastate marginalized communities that depend heavily on natural resources for their livelihoods. Farmers in drought-prone regions, for instance, face crop failures and loss of livestock, which can lead to severe economic distress and increased poverty. Similarly, communities that rely on fishing may find their income sources threatened by changing ocean temperatures and acidification, which affect fish populations and ecosystems.

Moreover, the economic impact extends beyond immediate livelihoods. Disasters such as hurricanes and floods can destroy homes and community infrastructure, leading to long-term displacement and financial instability. Recovery from such events is slower in marginalized communities due to limited access to insurance, savings, or credit facilities that would facilitate rebuilding and recovery.

Social and Cultural Impacts

Climate change can also have profound social and cultural impacts on marginalized groups. Displacement due to climate change can lead to the loss of ancestral lands and traditional knowledge, eroding cultural identities and community cohesion. For indigenous populations, whose way of life and cultural heritage are closely tied to their environment, this loss is particularly devastating.

Additionally, climate-induced migration can lead to overcrowding in urban areas, straining infrastructure and increasing competition for jobs, housing, and services. This often results in heightened social tensions and can exacerbate existing inequalities and discrimination against marginalized groups.

Barriers to Adaptation and Mitigation

Despite being most at risk, marginalized communities frequently face substantial barriers to participating in climate change adaptation and mitigation efforts. Lack of political power, economic resources, and access to technology and information can prevent these communities from implementing effective climate responses.

Furthermore, traditional top-down approaches to climate change policy can fail to address the specific needs and circumstances of marginalized groups. This oversight can lead to the implementation of solutions that are not only ineffective but sometimes harmful to these communities, reinforcing cycles of vulnerability and exclusion.

Empowering Marginalized Communities

Addressing the impact of climate change on marginalized communities requires empowering them through inclusive and equitable climate action. This means involving these communities in the decision-making processes and ensuring they have access to the resources needed to adapt to and mitigate the effects of climate change.

Community-based adaptation strategies can be particularly effective, as they leverage local knowledge and foster community ownership of climate solutions. These strategies might include sustainable agricultural practices, community-managed disaster risk reduction, or locally managed renewable energy projects.

International and national policies must also prioritize social equity and justice in climate action to address the disproportionate impacts on marginalized groups. Financial investments, such as climate financing for adaptation projects, need to be accessible to these communities. Moreover, legal frameworks should protect the rights of marginalized populations to land, water, and other resources crucial for their resilience.

The disproportionate impact of climate change on marginalized communities is a stark reminder of the global inequalities that pervade our societies. It underscores the need for a concerted, global effort to address these disparities through robust, community-informed, and inclusive climate action. By focusing on the vulnerabilities and capacities of these groups, and ensuring they have a voice in the climate dialogue, we can work towards a more just and sustainable future for all.

ᐅᐅᐅ

"Corporate responsibility in the realm of
sustainability is about aligning business practices
with the global necessity for environmental
integrity and social equity."

ᗡᗡᗡ

THIRTEEN

EDUCATION FOR SUSTAINABILITY: LEARNING TO LIVE DIFFERENTLY

Education for sustainability is a transformative process that not only encompasses the integration of sustainable principles into teaching and learning but also aims to inspire and equip individuals with the understanding and skills necessary to shape a sustainable future. This educational approach addresses the interdependence of environmental protection, economic health, and social equity, fostering a holistic understanding and responsible action among individuals and communities.

Redefining the Purpose of Education

Traditionally, education has been viewed primarily as a means to attain personal success and economic advancement. However, education for sustainability redefines this purpose, emphasizing the development of knowledge, skills, and values that promote the sustainability of the environment, economy, and societies. This shift involves a comprehensive rethinking of curriculum and pedagogy to include critical thinking about sustainability challenges such as climate change, resource depletion, and social inequality.

Integrating Sustainability into Curriculum

One of the fundamental aspects of education for sustainability is the integration of its concepts across all disciplines. This isn't confined to environmental science; it extends to economics, arts, humanities, and beyond. For instance, students in economics might study the principles of sustainable development and circular economies, while literature classes might explore themes of environmental justice or human relationships with nature.

Curricula designed around sustainability also encourage interdisciplinary learning, reflecting the interconnected nature of today's global challenges. This approach helps students make connections between subjects and understand complex systems, fostering a deeper understanding of how societal choices impact the environment and vice versa.

Developing Critical Thinking and Problem-Solving Skills

Education for sustainability emphasizes critical thinking, problem-solving, and participatory learning. Students are encouraged to question and explore how human activities affect the planet and to devise viable solutions to real-world problems. This might involve project-based learning that includes community service projects, sustainability audits of school facilities, or collaborative research projects that address local environmental issues.

For example, students might work on projects that require them to create sustainable business models, design renewable energy solutions, or develop water conservation programs. These activities not only enhance learning but also encourage students to apply their knowledge in practical, impactful ways.

Fostering Global Citizenship and Ethical Awareness

Educating for sustainability also involves cultivating global citizenship, preparing students to engage with the world as informed, ethical, and active citizens. This includes an appreciation for diversity, an understanding of global interdependencies, and a sense of responsibility to act locally while thinking globally. Through this lens, students learn to see themselves as part of a larger ecosystem and are motivated to make decisions that contribute positively to that system.

Ethical awareness is also critical, as it underpins decisions about how to live sustainably. Education systems can foster this by incorporating discussions about ethics, equity, and justice in the context of sustainability. Students learn to consider not only how decisions affect the environment but also how they impact different populations around the world.

Lifelong Learning and Community Engagement

Education for sustainability recognizes that learning does not end in the classroom. It promotes lifelong learning and encourages individuals to stay informed about scientific and societal advancements related to sustainability. Adults and children alike are urged to continue educating themselves through informal learning opportunities such as community workshops, online courses, and educational media.

Community engagement is another crucial element, as it allows learners to apply their skills and knowledge in real-world settings. Schools and universities can play a pivotal role by partnering with local governments, businesses, and NGOs to facilitate projects that allow students to work on practical sustainability initiatives. This not only enhances learning but also helps students feel connected to their communities and empowers them to make a difference.

Scaling and Adapting Education for Sustainability

The scalability of education for sustainability is vital for its widespread impact. This requires commitment at all levels of governance—from local schools to international educational policies. Teachers and educators need training and resources to effectively deliver sustainability education, and institutions must be supported to integrate these principles into their core operations.

Furthermore, technology can play a significant role in scaling sustainability education. Digital platforms can facilitate the sharing of resources, collaboration across borders, and the dissemination of innovative teaching practices. This can help democratize education for sustainability, making it accessible to a broader audience worldwide.

Education for sustainability is a dynamic and expansive approach to learning that prepares individuals to navigate and shape a world where environmental, economic, and social systems are rapidly changing. By fostering a deep understanding of sustainability issues, critical thinking skills, and a commitment to ethical action, education for sustainability empowers individuals to contribute to a more sustainable and equitable world. Through continual learning and community involvement, it encourages a cultural shift towards sustainability that can permeate all levels of society.

ᐁᐁᐁ

"Activism and advocacy are the voices of the planet,
echoing through communities and across time
zones, urging us to act before it is too late."

ᗡᗡᗡ

FOURTEEN

TECHNOLOGY AND INNOVATION FOR A GREENER TOMORROW

In the face of global environmental challenges, technology and innovation emerge as pivotal forces driving the transition towards a more sustainable and greener future. Harnessing the power of advanced technologies can lead to significant improvements in energy efficiency, waste reduction, and resource management, contributing to environmental conservation and the mitigation of climate change impacts. This comprehensive exploration delves into the various technological advancements and innovative solutions reshaping our approach to sustainability.

Renewable Energy Technologies

One of the most critical areas where technology plays a transformative role is in the generation and utilization of renewable energy. Innovations in solar, wind, hydroelectric, and geothermal technologies have dramatically increased their efficiency and reduced costs, making renewable energy more accessible and affordable than ever before. For instance, advancements in photovoltaic materials have led to higher solar panel efficiencies, while enhanced turbine designs have improved wind energy capture.

Battery technology, crucial for energy storage, has seen significant breakthroughs, particularly in lithium-ion and solid-state batteries. These developments are crucial for stabilizing the intermittent nature of solar and wind energies, allowing for more reliable energy supply systems. Furthermore, smart grid technology integrates digital communications technology with power networks, enhancing the efficiency and reliability of energy distribution and enabling the integration of distributed energy resources like rooftop solar.

Smart and Sustainable Cities

Technology also plays a crucial role in the development of smart and sustainable cities, which utilize IoT (Internet of Things) sensors, big data, and analytics to optimize resource use and improve sustainability. Smart city technologies help in managing traffic flows more efficiently, reducing energy consumption in buildings, monitoring air quality, and enhancing waste management through smart recycling bins that signal when they are full.

Urban planning software and GIS (Geographic Information Systems) technologies enable city planners to design urban environments that maximize green spaces, optimize building layouts for natural heating and lighting, and reduce the urban heat island effect. These tools help cities become more livable and environmentally friendly, directly benefiting both the planet and human well-being.

Precision Agriculture

In the agricultural sector, technology and innovation are revolutionizing the way food is grown, harvested, and distributed. Precision agriculture uses drones, satellite images, and IoT sensors to monitor crop health, soil quality, and water usage with great accuracy. This data-driven approach allows farmers to apply water, fertilizers, and pesticides more efficiently, reducing waste and environmental impact. Moreover, innovations such as vertical farming and hydroponics enable food production in urban settings, minimizing transportation emissions and promoting local food consumption.

Water Purification and Management

Technological advancements are also critical in managing and conserving water resources. New water purification technologies, including reverse osmosis and nanofiltration, allow for the effective treatment of wastewater, making water recycling more feasible for both industrial and domestic use. Smart irrigation systems can significantly reduce water usage in agriculture by delivering precise water amounts directly to the roots of plants, thereby conserving water.

Waste Management and Recycling Technologies

Innovations in waste management are transforming the recycling industry by improving the efficiency of resource recovery and reducing landfill use. Automated sorting technologies in recycling facilities can identify and separate different materials with high accuracy, increasing the quality and quantity of recyclable materials recovered. Furthermore, developments in chemical recycling technologies allow for the breakdown of plastics back into their original monomers, facilitating the creation of new plastic products without degradation of quality.

Sustainable Manufacturing and Materials

Technological innovation extends to the development of sustainable manufacturing processes and materials. For instance, the use of AI and machine learning in manufacturing optimizes production processes to minimize waste and energy use. Additionally, the development of biodegradable plastics and environmentally friendly materials such as mycelium-based products provides sustainable alternatives that reduce environmental impacts associated with traditional materials.

The role of technology and innovation in driving sustainability is expansive and dynamic. As the world continues to confront environmental challenges, the deployment of advanced technologies and innovative practices is crucial for achieving a greener, more sustainable future. These technologies not only address immediate environmental concerns but also offer pathways for long-term sustainable growth, fundamentally altering our interaction with the planet's resources. By continuing to invest in and develop these technologies, society can move closer to achieving the environmental, economic, and social pillars of sustainability.

ﬤﬤﬤ

"Legal frameworks for sustainability must do more than enforce; they must empower, giving voice to the voiceless and strength to the stewards of our environment."

ᗡᗡᗡ

FIFTEEN

GOVERNMENT POLICIES AND GREEN LEGISLATION

Government policies and green legislation play a critical role in shaping the trajectory towards a sustainable future. These regulatory frameworks and incentives are essential for guiding both public and private sectors in their environmental responsibilities and for fostering practices that contribute to sustainability. The effectiveness of such policies and legislation is often seen in their ability to address complex environmental challenges, promote green technologies, and ensure equitable outcomes for all segments of society.

Framework for Environmental Protection

Environmental policies and green legislation create a framework for protecting natural resources and reducing pollution. These laws typically cover a wide range of areas, including air quality, water quality, waste management, and biodiversity conservation. For example, regulations like the Clean Air Act and Clean Water Act in the United States have been instrumental in reducing air and water pollution levels, while the European Union's Natura 2000 network has worked to protect biodiversity across the continent.

These laws often set limits on the amount of pollutants that can be released into the environment and require industries to adopt cleaner technologies. Compliance is enforced through fines, penalties, or other legal actions, which help ensure that businesses operate within the bounds of environmental safety and sustainability.

Incentives for Renewable Energy and Efficiency

One of the most impactful areas of government policy relates to renewable energy and energy efficiency. Governments around the world have implemented a range of incentives to promote the adoption of renewable energy sources such as solar, wind, and biomass. These incentives can include tax breaks, subsidies, feed-in tariffs, and renewable energy certificates. For instance, Germany's Energiewende (energy transition) policy has been successful in significantly increasing the country's renewable energy capacity through a combination of subsidies and feed-in tariffs.

Similarly, policies aimed at improving energy efficiency are critical in reducing overall energy consumption and lowering greenhouse gas emissions. Programs like the Energy Star rating in the USA encourage manufacturers and consumers to choose more energy-efficient appliances, which help reduce electricity usage and environmental impact.

Sustainable Urban Development

Governments also play a pivotal role in promoting sustainable urban development through zoning laws, building codes, and urban planning policies. These regulations can dictate everything from the energy efficiency standards of buildings to the integration of green spaces in urban areas. Policies that encourage or mandate the construction of green buildings, such as those adhering to LEED standards, contribute significantly to reducing the carbon footprint of urban centers.

Moreover, transportation policies can influence urban sustainability by promoting public transit, cycling, and walking, while discouraging the use of fossil-fuel-driven vehicles through congestion pricing and high-emission vehicle taxes. These measures not only reduce urban air pollution but also improve the overall health and well-being of the population.

Conservation and Natural Resource Management

Legislation related to the conservation of natural resources and wildlife plays an essential role in sustainable management practices. This includes laws that regulate forestry practices, fishing quotas, and wildlife protection. Such policies ensure that natural resources are used sustainably and that biodiversity is preserved for future generations.

For example, the establishment of protected areas and national parks is a common legislative approach to conserving biodiversity and natural landscapes. These areas not only protect ecosystems and species but also provide opportunities for scientific research and eco-tourism, which can further contribute to conservation efforts and local economies.

Adaptation to Climate Change

With the increasing impacts of climate change, governments are also focusing on policies aimed at adaptation. This includes measures to protect against sea-level rise, manage water resources more efficiently, and improve agricultural practices to cope with changing climatic conditions. Adaptation policies are particularly important for vulnerable communities that might lack the resources to respond effectively to climate hazards.

Public Participation and Transparency

Effective green legislation also involves ensuring public participation and transparency in environmental governance. This means that government decisions regarding environmental policy should be made with public input and be openly available for scrutiny. Such practices not only improve the legitimacy of policies but also enhance public awareness and education on environmental issues.

Government policies and green legislation are indispensable tools in the pursuit of sustainability. By setting standards, providing incentives, and enforcing laws, governments can steer their countries towards more sustainable practices. However, the success of these policies largely depends on their design, implementation, and the political and economic context in which they operate. As environmental challenges evolve, so too must the policies and legislation that address them, ensuring they remain effective in promoting a sustainable and equitable future for all.

ppp

"The tapestry of traditional knowledge, woven with modern science, creates a resilient framework for sustainable practices that honor both our heritage and our future."

❦❦❦

SIXTEEN
ACTIVISM AND ADVOCACY: VOICES FOR THE PLANET

Activism and advocacy play vital roles in the environmental movement, driving awareness, influencing policy, and mobilizing communities to protect the planet. These efforts range from local community actions to global campaigns and involve a diverse array of strategies including grassroots organizing, legal challenges, corporate campaigns, and policy advocacy. As the threats of climate change and environmental degradation continue to grow, the voices of activists and advocates have become more crucial than ever in pushing for substantial and sustained environmental action.

The Power of Grassroots Activism

Grassroots activism forms the backbone of environmental advocacy, drawing its strength from local communities and concerned citizens. These movements often start at a small scale but can grow to have a national or even global impact. One of the most powerful aspects of grassroots activism is its ability to engage and mobilize individuals who are directly affected by environmental issues, such as pollution, deforestation, or resource depletion.

Local movements have been instrumental in challenging environmentally destructive projects and policies. For example, community protests against deforestation or land grabs have often led to significant changes in local policies or even the abandonment of projects that would have had devastating environmental impacts. These movements not only protect local environments but also empower communities by giving them a voice in decisions that affect their lives and surroundings.

Legal Advocacy for Environmental Protection

Legal advocacy is another critical tool for environmental activism. Environmental lawyers and organizations often engage in litigation to enforce existing environmental laws or to challenge insufficient or harmful new policies and projects. Through the courts, advocates can achieve significant victories that not only create immediate change but also set legal precedents that benefit environmental protection efforts in the long run.

In many countries, legal battles have led to landmark decisions requiring governments to take more aggressive action on climate change. For instance, lawsuits filed by activists have forced governments to reevaluate and strengthen their carbon emission reduction targets. Legal advocacy also plays a crucial role in holding corporations accountable for pollution and environmental degradation, compelling them to adopt more sustainable practices.

Corporate Campaigns and Consumer Boycotts

Activism and advocacy also target corporations, urging them to adopt environmentally friendly practices. Through public campaigns, protests, and boycotts, activists can pressure companies to change their operations to be more sustainable. These efforts are often supported by extensive research and collaboration with environmental experts to ensure that demands are scientifically sound and feasible.

Consumer boycotts are a particularly effective form of corporate activism, as they directly impact a company's bottom line. By mobilizing consumers to avoid products that are harmful to the environment, activists can force companies to reconsider their practices. Additionally, positive campaigns that highlight green businesses can help shift market standards towards sustainability.

Policy Advocacy

Engaging with policymakers is essential for enacting environmental protections at a legislative level. Environmental advocates work to influence local, national, and international policies by providing expertise, drafting legislation, and mobilizing public support for environmental measures. This form of advocacy is crucial for establishing frameworks that ensure long-term environmental sustainability.

Advocates often work in coalitions to strengthen their influence and capacity to engage with policymakers. By collaborating with scientists, economists, and other experts, advocates can provide robust data and arguments that support the need for specific environmental policies. Public campaigns that mobilize voter support for these policies can also be decisive, particularly in democratic contexts where public opinion can shape political priorities.

Global Movements and International Advocacy

On the international stage, environmental activism takes the form of global movements and advocacy within international organizations. Activists and NGOs often collaborate across borders to address global environmental issues such as climate change, biodiversity loss, and pollution. These efforts are vital for pushing for international agreements and cooperation on environmental issues.

Global movements, such as those inspired by figures like Greta Thunberg, have brought unprecedented attention to climate change and have mobilized millions of people worldwide to demand action from their governments. International advocacy also plays a role in shaping global environmental agreements, such as the Paris Agreement, and in promoting international standards on environmental protection and sustainability.

Activism and advocacy are indispensable in the fight to protect the planet. Through local and global efforts, dedicated individuals and organizations are driving the environmental agenda forward, advocating for sustainable practices and policies, and holding governments and corporations accountable. As environmental challenges grow more complex and pressing, the role of activism and advocacy remains ever crucial, representing the voices and interests of the planet and its inhabitants. By continuing to advocate for environmental justice and sustainability, activists not only contribute to the health of the environment but also support the well-being of current and future generations.

ᗡᗡᗡ

"Sustainability is not a solo journey but a collective voyage, demanding cooperation across borders, sectors, and ideologies to create a truly sustainable world."

ᗡᗡᗡ

SEVENTEEN

Sustainable Cities: Urban Planning for the Future

Sustainable cities embody the intersection of urban development and environmental stewardship, seeking to minimize ecological footprints while enhancing the quality of life for their residents. As urban populations continue to grow at an unprecedented rate, the need for sustainable urban planning becomes increasingly urgent. This form of planning encompasses a broad spectrum of strategies, from green building and efficient infrastructure to policies that support social inclusion and economic vitality.

Integrating Sustainability into Urban Design

The core of sustainable urban planning involves the thoughtful integration of environmental considerations with urban development. This means designing cities that not only support economic and social activities but also contribute to the health of the environment. Sustainable urban design includes the implementation of green spaces, eco-friendly public transportation systems, energy-efficient buildings, and infrastructure that supports cycling and walking. These elements are crucial for reducing urban heat islands, managing stormwater, reducing greenhouse gas emissions, and improving public health and well-being.

Green Building and Energy Efficiency

A fundamental aspect of sustainable cities is the focus on green building practices and energy efficiency. Buildings are significant contributors to carbon emissions, mainly through heating, cooling, and electricity usage. Implementing stringent building codes that require or encourage energy efficiency can dramatically reduce a city's environmental impact. Features such as better insulation, energy-efficient windows, and green roofs can help buildings consume less energy and contribute to the overall sustainability of urban areas.

Moreover, integrating renewable energy sources like solar panels into building designs or community grids reduces reliance on fossil fuels and promotes energy independence. Urban planners are increasingly turning to smart grid technology to optimize energy use across cities, allowing for real-time adjustments in energy supply and demand.

Transportation and Mobility

Sustainable urban mobility is another critical component. Well-planned cities encourage the use of public transport, cycling, and walking as primary modes of transportation. Developing comprehensive networks of public transit, bike lanes, and pedestrian paths not only reduces traffic congestion and air pollution but also promotes healthier lifestyles. Additionally, policies promoting electric vehicles, including charging infrastructure and incentives for electric car purchasers, can further reduce urban emissions.

Water Management and Waste Reduction

Effective water management systems are essential in sustainable urban planning. This involves not only ensuring the sustainable use and reuse of water resources but also protecting against water pollution. Urban areas can adopt systems for rainwater harvesting and greywater reuse, which reduce the demand on freshwater supplies and decrease the burden on municipal water systems.

Waste reduction and management are equally important. Cities that implement comprehensive recycling and composting programs can significantly decrease the amount of waste sent to landfills. Furthermore, promoting waste-to-energy plants can help cities manage waste while generating energy, thus hitting two birds with one stone.

Social Equity and Inclusive Planning

Sustainability also entails social equity and inclusivity. This means planning cities in ways that all residents—regardless of their economic status—have access to essential services, healthy living conditions, and opportunities for economic participation. Affordable housing policies, equitable access to community resources like parks and schools, and inclusive decision-making processes are all vital for creating cities that are truly sustainable.

Adapting to Climate Change

Urban areas are particularly vulnerable to climate change impacts such as heatwaves, flooding, and sea-level rise. Sustainable urban planning must, therefore, include strategies for adaptation. This can involve enhancing the resilience of infrastructure, designing flood defenses, and implementing heat action plans. Cities must plan for these changes proactively to protect their populations and infrastructure from climate-related damages.

Smart Cities and Technological Innovations

The concept of smart cities integrates information and communication technologies into urban management, which can significantly enhance the efficiency of urban operations and services. Smart technologies can help manage everything from traffic and public transport to energy use and municipal services, making cities more efficient and reducing their environmental impact.

Sustainable urban planning is an expansive field that encompasses a wide range of practices and strategies aimed at making cities livable, environmentally friendly, and economically viable. As cities continue to grow, the implementation of sustainable urban planning principles will be crucial for ensuring that urban development supports both the health of the planet and the well-being of its inhabitants. By focusing on green infrastructure, efficient resource use, and inclusive policies, cities can lead the way towards a more sustainable future.

ррр

"In our hands lies the power to mold a sustainable
future, through the choices we make every
day—from the products we buy to the energy we
consume."

ууу

EIGHTEEN

THE ROLE OF ART AND CULTURE IN SUSTAINABILITY

Art and culture play transformative roles in promoting sustainability, offering unique ways to inspire, educate, and mobilize communities around environmental issues. While often overlooked in technical discussions of sustainability, the integration of artistic and cultural dimensions can deepen public understanding of environmental challenges and foster a more profound connection to the natural world. By engaging people's emotions and imaginations, art and culture can drive meaningful change and support the development of sustainable practices that resonate with diverse communities.

Art as a Medium for Environmental Awareness

Artists across various mediums—painting, sculpture, installation, literature, music, and performance—have the power to make abstract environmental issues tangible and immediate to their audiences. Through their work, artists can visualize complex data, depict future scenarios, and present stark reflections or beautiful homages to nature, which can be instrumental in shifting public perceptions about the environment.

Environmental art, in particular, directly engages with ecological issues through creative expressions that aim to raise awareness or provoke action. Whether it's through large-scale installations that highlight the problem of plastic pollution in the oceans or through performances that dramatize the impact of climate change, environmental art can make environmental issues more accessible and emotionally impactful.

Cultural Practices and Sustainability

Traditional cultural practices often embody principles of sustainability, honed over centuries of interaction with the local environment. Many indigenous and rural communities live in ways that are inherently sustainable, guided by cultural norms and practices that respect natural resources and understand the limits of their environment. These practices can offer modern societies valuable lessons in sustainability, such as crop rotation, water conservation, and the use of indigenous plants for food and medicine.

Preserving these cultural practices and integrating their wisdom into contemporary sustainability efforts is crucial. It not only helps maintain biodiversity and ecological balance but also ensures the survival of cultural heritage that can continue to teach future generations.

Sustainable Design and Architecture

Culture and art also influence sustainable design and architecture, which considers the environmental impact of human-made structures and seeks to minimize this impact through innovative and thoughtful design. Sustainable architecture uses locally sourced, recycled, or renewable materials and incorporates energy-efficient technologies and natural elements, reducing the carbon footprint of buildings and enhancing their aesthetic and functional qualities.

Moreover, sustainable design extends to fashion, furniture, and everyday objects, which can be produced in environmentally friendly ways that challenge the often wasteful consumer culture. Designers and artists play a pivotal role in this field, creating objects and spaces that are not only functional and beautiful but also environmentally conscious.

Cultural Festivals and Environmental Campaigns

Cultural events and festivals can be powerful platforms for spreading sustainability messages. By embedding environmental themes into cultural celebrations, organizers can educate large audiences in engaging and impactful ways. These events often feature activities such as workshops, art installations, and discussions that focus on sustainability, alongside entertainment.

Additionally, many cultural institutions, such as museums, theaters, and concert halls, are increasingly engaging in sustainability. They adopt green practices in their operations and programming, thus setting an example for other institutions and their visitors.

The Role of Media and Entertainment in Shaping Perceptions

The broader media and entertainment industries also have significant roles in shaping cultural perceptions of sustainability. Films, television shows, and online content that focus on environmental issues can reach vast audiences and have a profound impact on public awareness and attitudes. Environmental documentaries, for instance, have been instrumental in bringing issues like global warming, wildlife conservation, and pollution to the forefront of public consciousness.

Engagement and Community Action

Art and culture not only raise awareness but also engage communities in environmental action. Community art projects can involve residents in creating works that beautify neighborhoods while promoting environmental messages. These projects can strengthen community ties and encourage collective actions such as neighborhood clean-ups, tree plantings, and community gardening efforts, fostering a sense of pride and stewardship for the local environment.

The role of art and culture in sustainability is multifaceted and profound. By connecting the environmental, social, and economic aspects of sustainability, art and culture can reach people on a deeply personal level, inspiring change and fostering a greater connection to the environment. As the world continues to grapple with environmental challenges, the integration of artistic and cultural perspectives in sustainability efforts offers innovative pathways to a more sustainable future, making these endeavors not only more effective but also more inclusive.

ᗞᗞᗞ

"The hidden path to ethical sustainability requires us to look beyond immediate conveniences and embrace practices that ensure long-term health for our planet."

ꝏꝏꝏ

NINETEEN

GLOBAL PARTNERSHIPS FOR ENVIRONMENTAL JUSTICE

Global partnerships for environmental justice are essential in addressing the complex and interrelated issues of environmental degradation, social inequality, and economic disparity. These partnerships, which span across nations, sectors, and cultures, aim to ensure that environmental benefits and burdens are shared equitably and that all individuals, regardless of their background, have access to a clean and healthy environment. The success of such partnerships depends on collaboration between governments, international organizations, civil society, the private sector, and communities, particularly those most affected by environmental injustices.

The Foundation of Environmental Justice

Environmental justice is grounded in the belief that all people have the right to an environment that does not harm their health or well-being and that they should have a voice in the decisions that affect their environment. This principle challenges the traditional models of development that often place environmental burdens on marginalized communities while distributing benefits such as clean air, water, and access to natural resources to more affluent or politically powerful groups.

The Role of International Agreements and Conventions

One of the most critical components of global partnerships for environmental justice is the establishment and enforcement of international environmental agreements. Treaties such as the Paris Agreement on climate change, the Convention on Biological Diversity, and the Basel Convention on the control of transboundary movements of hazardous wastes play a pivotal role in setting global standards and commitments. These agreements ensure that countries adhere to principles that protect the environment and promote fairness and equity in the distribution of environmental risks and benefits.

Strengthening International Governance

Effective global partnerships require robust international governance structures that can oversee and enforce environmental agreements. Organizations like the United Nations Environment Programme (UNEP) and the World Health Organization (WHO) are key players in international environmental governance. These organizations not only provide a platform for negotiation and agreement but also offer technical assistance, capacity building, and monitoring to ensure that commitments are met.

Collaboration Across Borders

Environmental justice issues often transcend national boundaries, making international cooperation essential. Pollution, climate change, and biodiversity loss are global challenges that require coordinated responses. Global partnerships facilitate shared strategies, resources, and knowledge, enhancing the ability of individual countries and communities to address these issues effectively.

For instance, transboundary conservation efforts that protect shared ecosystems and wildlife corridors between countries can be more effective than isolated actions.

Empowering Local and Indigenous Communities

For global partnerships to be truly effective in promoting environmental justice, they must empower the communities most affected by environmental issues. This involves supporting local and indigenous rights to manage and protect their natural resources.

Indigenous peoples often have a deep connection to and knowledge of their environments, making them invaluable partners in conservation and environmental management.

Incorporating traditional ecological knowledge into global environmental strategies not only helps protect biodiversity but also respects and strengthens the cultural heritage of indigenous populations.

Partnerships like the Indigenous Peoples Alliance for Rights and Development aim to create frameworks for empowering indigenous communities worldwide by integrating their perspectives and knowledge into global environmental decision-making processes.

Role of Non-Governmental Organizations (NGOs)

NGOs play a crucial role in building and sustaining global

partnerships for environmental justice. They act as advocates for marginalized communities, watchdogs that hold governments and corporations accountable, and educators who raise awareness about environmental justice issues.

Organizations such as Greenpeace, the World Wildlife Fund, and local advocacy groups bring attention to injustices and mobilize public and political support for equitable environmental policies.

Corporate Responsibility and Private Sector Engagement

The private sector also has a significant role in advancing environmental justice through global partnerships. Companies can adopt sustainable practices that reduce environmental impact and improve community well-being. Corporate social responsibility (CSR) initiatives that focus on equitable resource management, pollution reduction, and community engagement are essential.

Furthermore, businesses can collaborate through partnerships like the United Nations Global Compact to share best practices and strengthen their commitments to environmental justice.

Education and Capacity Building

Education is a powerful tool in promoting environmental justice globally. Educational initiatives that focus on environmental ethics, sustainability, and justice can cultivate a new generation of leaders equipped to deal with complex global challenges.

Capacity building, particularly in developing countries, ensures that communities have the skills and resources to advocate for and implement just and sustainable environmental practices.

Global partnerships for environmental justice are crucial for addressing the interconnected challenges of environmental degradation, social inequality, and economic disparity. By fostering cooperation across nations and sectors, supporting the rights and participation of affected communities, and ensuring equitable distribution of environmental benefits and burdens, these partnerships pave the way for a more just and sustainable world.

As the planet faces increasing environmental pressures, the commitment to strengthening and expanding these partnerships will be key to achieving long-lasting and equitable environmental solutions.

ÞÞÞ

"A greener tomorrow is crafted today through our actions—let us choose wisely, act boldly, and inspire others to join us in our mission for sustainability."

❦❦❦

TWENTY

LOOKING AHEAD: THE FUTURE OF ETHICAL SUSTAINABILITY

As we navigate the complexities of the 21st century, the concept of ethical sustainability becomes increasingly crucial. This forward-thinking approach integrates ethical considerations into sustainability, ensuring that our efforts to protect the planet are also aligned with principles of justice, equity, and respect for all beings. The future of ethical sustainability lies in a multifaceted approach that encompasses environmental integrity, social equity, and economic viability, all guided by moral principles that prioritize long-term well-being over short-term gains.

Integrating Ethics in Environmental Decision-Making

The core of ethical sustainability is the integration of ethical values into environmental decision-making. This involves considering the impacts of actions not only on the current population but also on future generations. It requires a shift from a purely utilitarian view of nature as a resource to be exploited, to a more holistic view that respects nature as a community to which we belong. This shift implies a profound respect for biodiversity and an acknowledgment of humanity's responsibility to protect and preserve the natural world for its intrinsic value and for the benefit of future generations.

Advancements in Green Technology and Innovation

Technological innovation plays a pivotal role in the future of ethical sustainability. Advances in renewable energy, such as solar, wind, and geothermal, continue to reduce our dependence on fossil fuels, decreasing our carbon footprint and mitigating the impact of climate change. Innovations in biotechnology, including the development of bio-based materials and the enhancement of agricultural practices, have the potential to reduce waste and improve food security without harming the environment.

Furthermore, the integration of AI and big data in environmental management can enhance our ability to monitor ecosystems, predict environmental changes, and manage resources more efficiently and ethically. These technologies can help ensure that environmental policies are based on accurate data and that they effectively address the most pressing environmental challenges.

Strengthening Global Governance and International Cooperation

Ethical sustainability requires strong global governance and international cooperation. As environmental issues do not respect national borders, international agreements and policies must be enforced to address global challenges like climate change, ocean acidification, and biodiversity loss. Strengthening institutions such as the United Nations Environment Programme (UNEP) and the Intergovernmental Panel on Climate Change (IPCC) is essential for fostering collaboration among nations and ensuring that environmental governance is fair, transparent, and accountable.

Promoting Social Equity and Environmental Justice

Ethical sustainability must also address social inequalities that are often exacerbated by environmental problems. This involves ensuring that all communities, particularly the most vulnerable and marginalized, have access to clean air, water, and land, and are protected from environmental hazards. Policies must be designed to distribute the benefits of sustainability initiatives equitably and to ensure that no group bears an undue share of environmental burdens.

Empowering local communities, especially indigenous peoples who often have a deep understanding of and respect for natural ecosystems, is crucial. Their involvement in conservation and sustainability practices not only helps preserve biodiversity but also supports the cultural diversity that enriches our global community.

Cultivating an Ethical Culture through Education and Awareness

Education is fundamental to fostering a culture of ethical sustainability. By integrating sustainability and ethics into educational curricula at all levels, from primary schools to universities, we can develop a new generation of citizens and leaders who are deeply committed to sustainable and ethical practices. Educational initiatives should focus on raising awareness about the interconnectedness of ecological, social, and economic systems and promoting values such as responsibility, respect, and compassion.

The Role of Businesses and the Economy

The business sector has a significant influence on sustainability and must be actively involved in promoting ethical practices. This involves adopting sustainable business models that prioritize long-term environmental health and social well-being over short-term profits. Companies should implement transparent and sustainable supply chains, reduce waste, and innovate products that contribute to sustainability.

Additionally, the concept of the circular economy, where resources are reused, recycled, and kept in circulation for as long as possible, presents a sustainable alternative to the traditional linear economy. Adopting circular economy principles can significantly reduce environmental impact and drive economic growth that is both sustainable and ethical.

Looking ahead, the future of ethical sustainability lies in our ability to integrate deep ethical considerations into all aspects of our interactions with the environment. By aligning technological advancements, international cooperation, social equity, and economic practices with ethical sustainability, we can forge a path that respects and preserves the earth while promoting a just society for today and for future generations. The journey towards ethical sustainability is complex and challenging but ultimately essential for the enduring health and prosperity of our planet and its inhabitants.

ppp

"Every effort toward sustainability is a stitch in the quilt of conservation, binding together the legacy of our past with the promise of our future."

❥❥❥

Citation And References

This book represents the culmination of extensive research and meticulous analysis, incorporating a diverse range of sources, including numerous books, scholarly studies, and personal experiences. Additionally, I have scoured various websites to gather relevant information and data essential for the compilation of this work. I have taken every precaution to ensure the accuracy of the information presented and have diligently cited all sources to acknowledge their contributions.

Despite these efforts, the possibility of inadvertent errors remains. I deeply value the insights of my readers and appreciate any feedback that can help identify and rectify such inaccuracies. I encourage you to bring any discrepancies to my attention.

Your feedback is not only welcome but crucial, as it will aid in correcting current editions and enhancing the content of future ones. I am committed to maintaining the highest standards of accuracy and reliability in my work and thank you for your support and understanding.

Additionally, I firmly uphold the principle of freedom of speech and expression as guaranteed under Article 19(1)(a) of the Constitution of India, and I respect the diverse viewpoints and expressions of all readers.

ppp

Other Books Of The Author

1. Empowering Minds: A Journey into Women's Self-Discovery and Power
2. The Dynamics of Motivation: Catalyzing Thought into Action
3. Meditation and Mental Well Being: The Path to Inner Peace and Clarity
4. The Psychology of Child Education: Nurturing Future Generations
5. Ethical Enlightenment: A Modern Guide to Living with Integrity
6. Voices of Empowerment: Stories of Women Rising Against Odds
7. Social Psychology in Everyday Life: Understanding Human Connections
8. The Essence of Motivational Speaking: Inspiring Change in Others
9. Balancing Acts: Women, Work, and the Will to Lead
10. Guiding with Grace: Raising Children with Compassion and Awareness
11. The Power of Positive Aging: Embracing Life After Fifty
12. Building Resilient Communities: Social Work in Action
13. The Ethical Educator: Principles for Teaching and Learning
14. From Insight to Impact: Social Psychology for a Better World
15. The Ethics of Empathy: A Guide to Ethical Living
16. The Science of Empowering the Self: Navigating Life's Challenges with Psychological Wisdom
17. The Mindful Conscious Leader: Meditation Techniques for Modern Management
18. Pioneering Spirit: Women's Pathways to Leadership and Empowerment
19. Feeling to Healing: The Role of Emotional Intelligence in Child Development
20. Transformative Talks and Words of Inspiration: Insights into Motivational Oratory

❧❧❧

Contact

Dr. Minakshi Bansal
Social Activist
Ahmedabad, Gujarat, Bharat
minakshiindiag20@yahoo.com

ᙠᙠᙠ

|| LOKAHA SAMASTHAHA SUKHINO BHAVANTU ||

• 131 •

|| LOKAHA SAMASTHAHA SUKHINO BHAVANTU ||

www.ingramcontent.com/pod-product-compliance
Lightning Source LLC
Chambersburg PA
CBHW020546160726

47991CB00002B/612